CHRISTMAS POP FAVORITES
for Piano Solo

ISBN 978-1-70516-918-6

Exclusively Distributed By

WILLIS MUSIC   Hal•LEONARD®

Visit Hal Leonard Online at
www.halleonard.com

World headquarters, contact:
Hal Leonard
7777 West Bluemound Road
Milwaukee, WI 53213
Email: info@halleonard.com

In Europe, contact:
Hal Leonard Europe Limited
1 Red Place
London, W1K 6PL
Email: info@halleonardeurope.com

In Australia, contact:
Hal Leonard Australia Pty. Ltd.
4 Lentara Court
Cheltenham, Victoria, 3192 Australia
Email: info@halleonard.com.au

These heartwarming seasonal favorites
were created by nine composers/arrangers of varying
backgrounds. They may be used for lessons,
as cocktail music, for recitals, or intimate gatherings.
Improvisations are encouraged.

A very merry Christmas

FROM WILLIS MUSIC

Contents

Blue Christmas

Words and Music by Billy Hayes
and Jay Johnson
Arranged by Melanie Spanswick

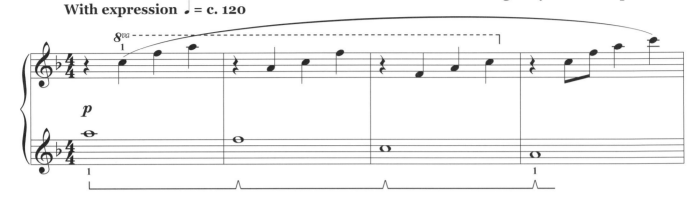

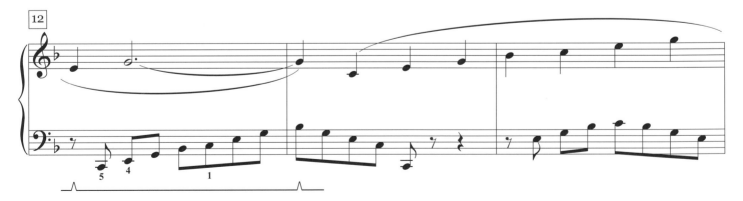

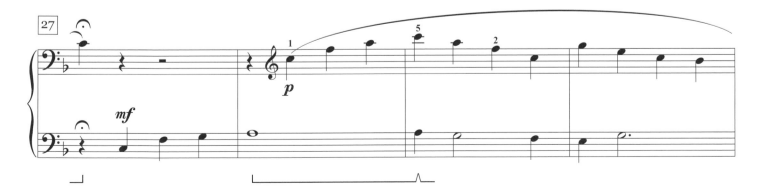

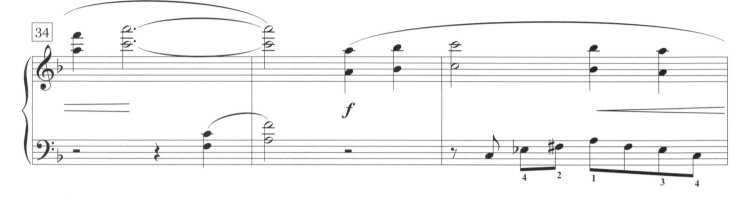

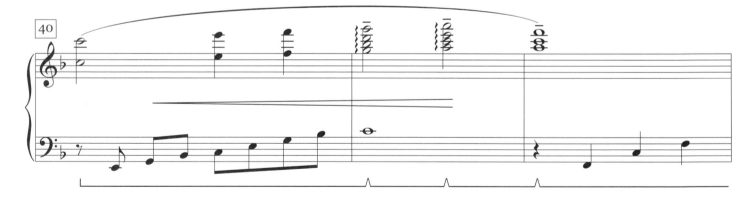

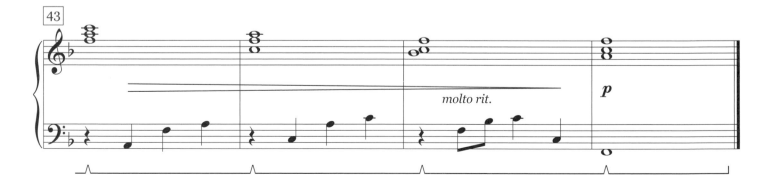

Frosty the Snow Man

Words and Music by Steve Nelson
and Jack Rollins
Arranged by Carolyn C. Setliff

Cheerfully, with a lilt

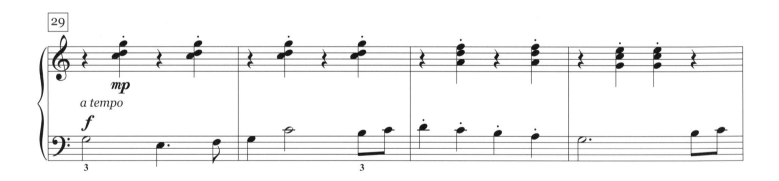

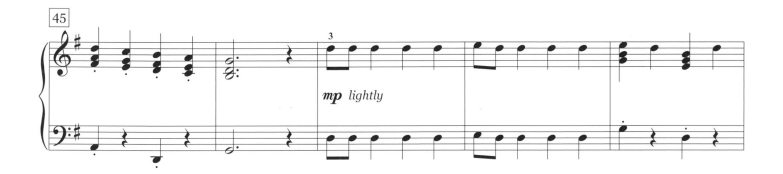

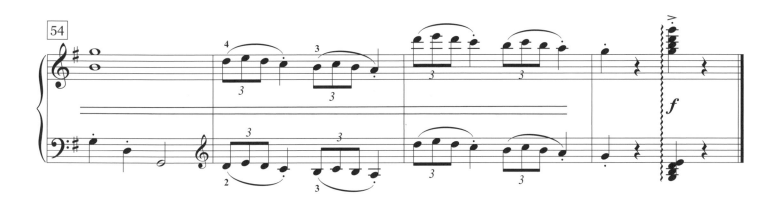

The Chipmunk Song

Words and Music by
Ross Bagdasarian
Arranged by Carolyn C. Setliff

Like a grand waltz

Christmas Time Is Here

from A CHARLIE BROWN CHRISTMAS

Words by Lee Mendelson
Music by Vince Guaraldi
Arranged by Melody Bober

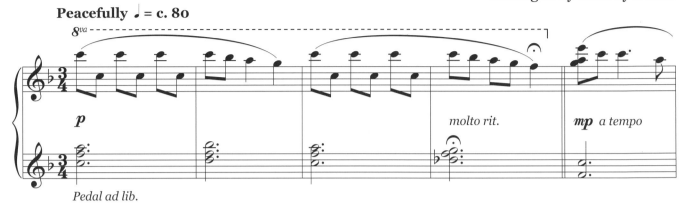

Do You Want to Build a Snowman?

from FROZEN

Music and Lyrics by Kristen Anderson-Lopez
and Robert Lopez
Arranged by Jason Sifford

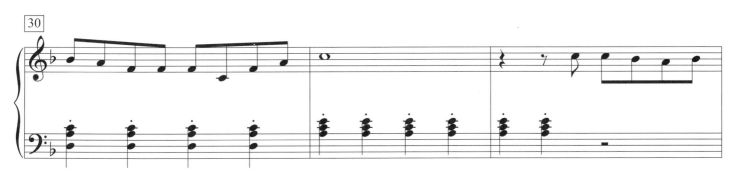

* Pianists with smaller hands may leave the top notes off of the 3-note chords.

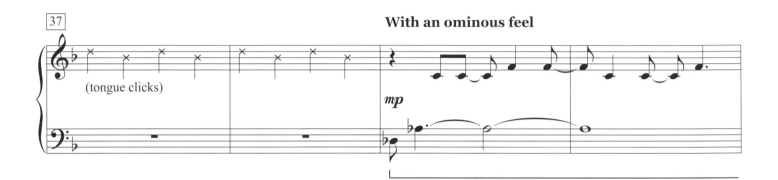

With an ominous feel

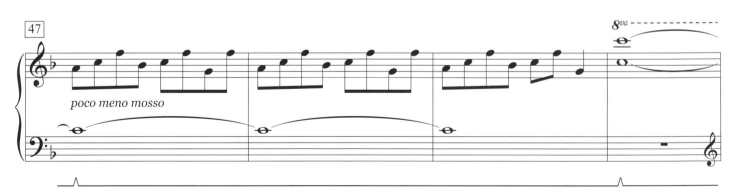

Slower, wistful ♩ = c. 88

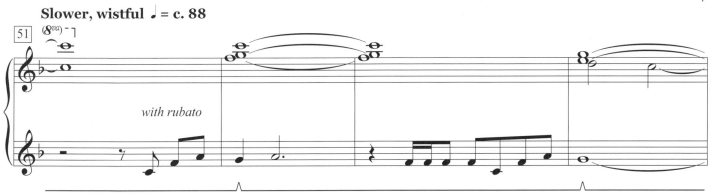

with rubato

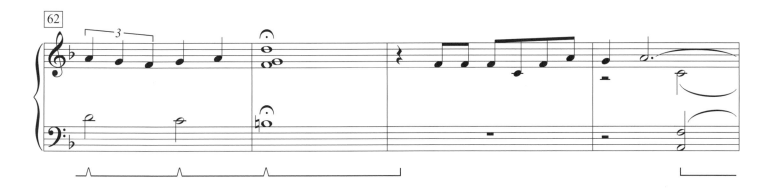

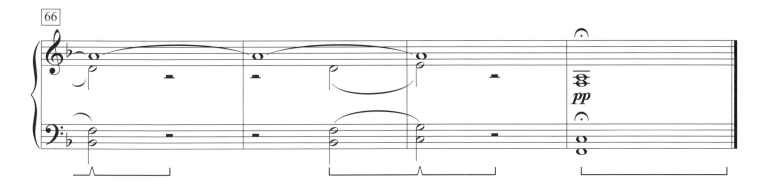

pp

Feliz Navidad

Music and Lyrics by
José Feliciano
Arranged by Glenda Austin

Festively, with exaggerated rhythms

Happy Holiday

from the Motion Picture Irving Berlin's HOLIDAY INN

Words and Music by
Irving Berlin
Arranged by Jason Sifford

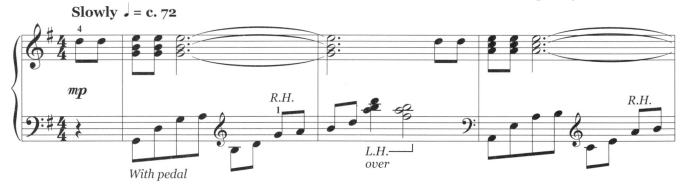

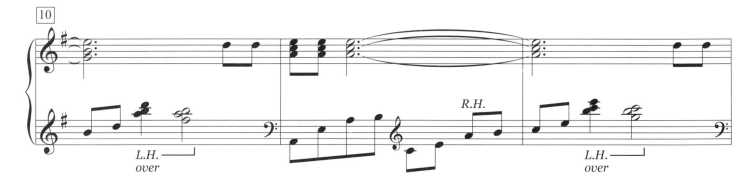

Allegro, lightly swung ♩ = c. 126

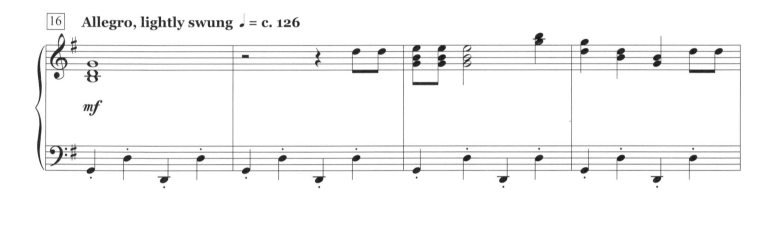

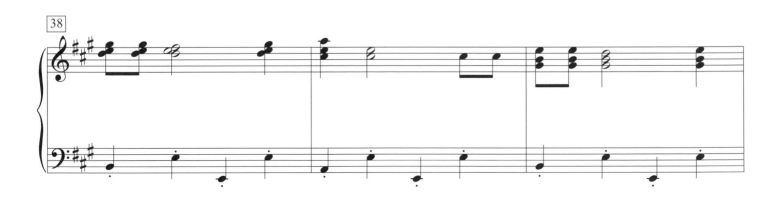

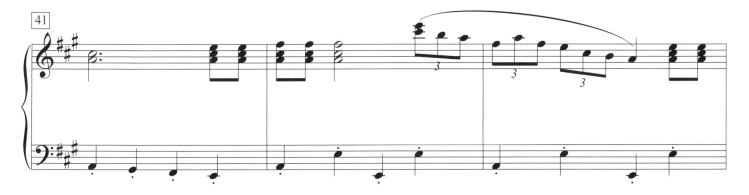

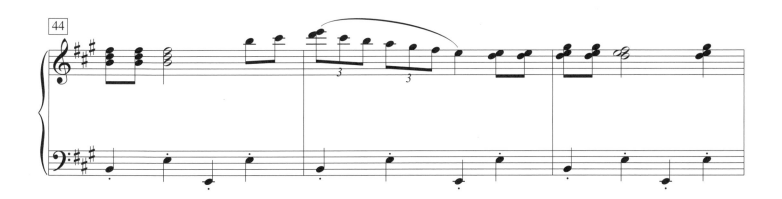

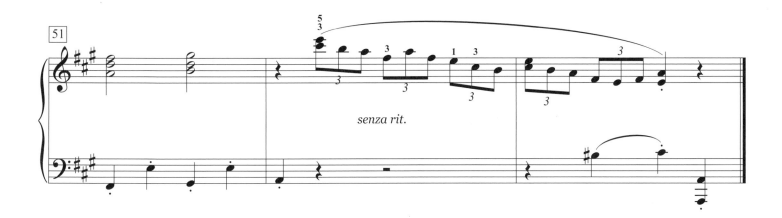

Have Yourself a Merry Little Christmas

from MEET ME IN ST. LOUIS

Words and Music by Hugh Martin
and Ralph Blane
Arranged by Naoko Ikeda

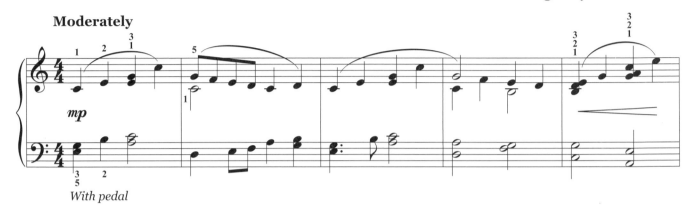

A Holly Jolly Christmas

Music and Lyrics by
Johnny Marks
Arranged by Randall Hartsell

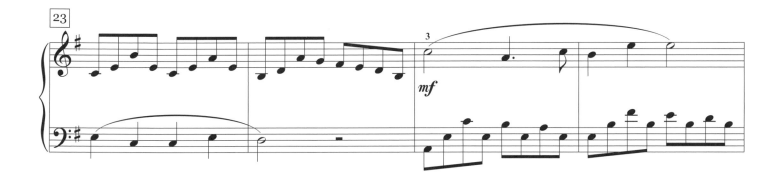

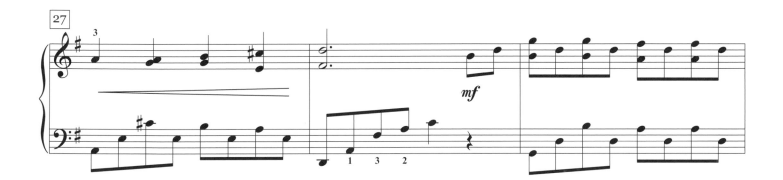

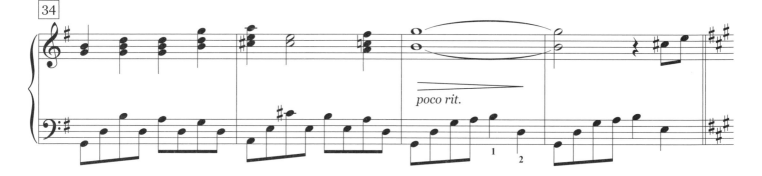

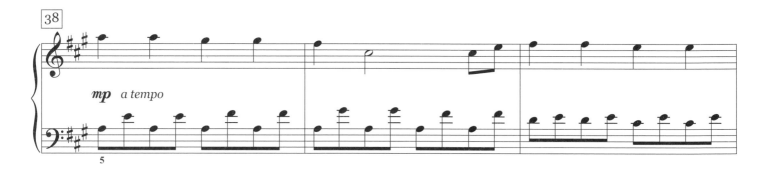

Mary, Did You Know?

Words and Music by Mark Lowry
and Buddy Greene
Arranged by Eric Baumgartner

Gently, with rubato

With pedal (sempre legato)

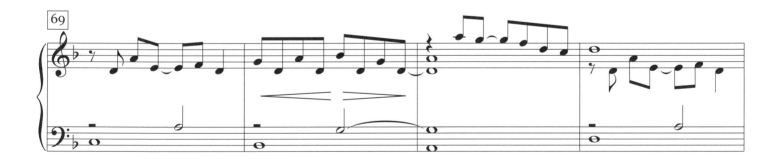

Mele Kalikimaka

Words and Music by
R. Alex Anderson
Arranged by Randall Hartsell

Slowly and freely

Lively and relaxed

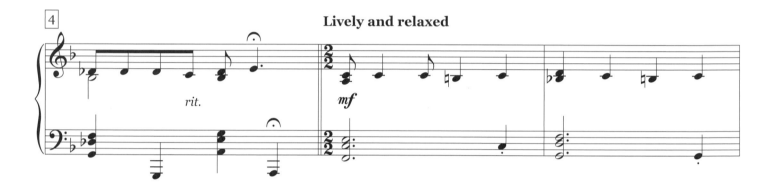

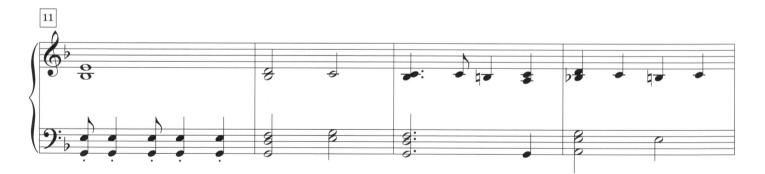

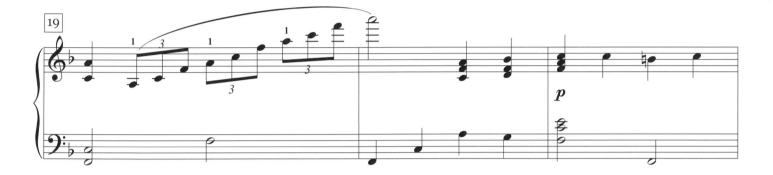

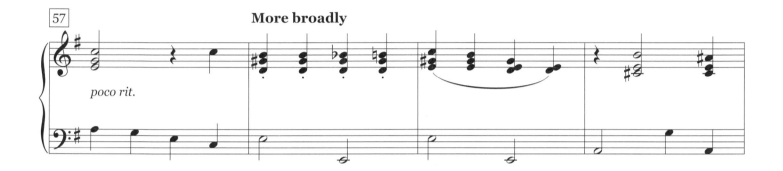

Merry Christmas, Darling

Words and Music by Richard Carpenter
and Frank Pooler
Arranged by Carolyn Miller

Rubato, with feeling

With pedal

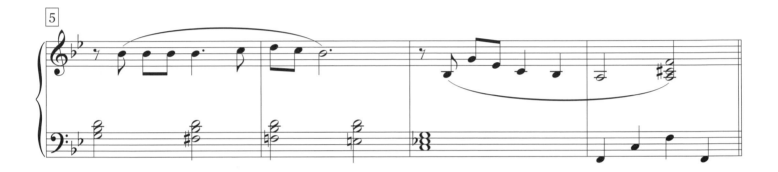

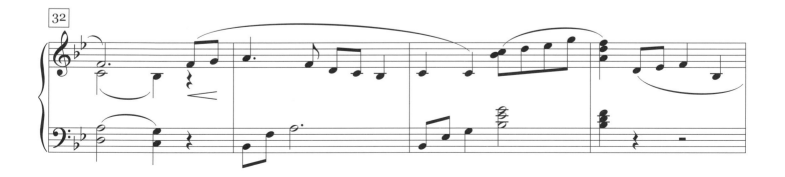

42

River

Words and Music by
Joni Mitchell
Arranged by Eric Baumgartner

Moderately

With pedal (sempre legato)

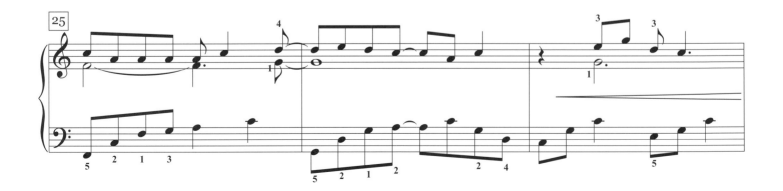

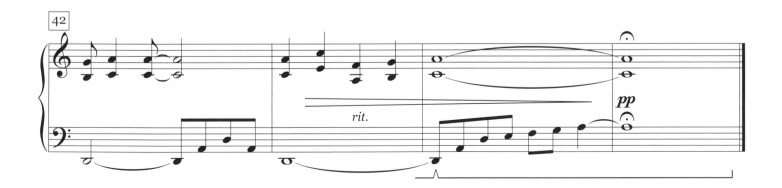

Silver Bells
from the Paramount Picture THE LEMON DROP KID

Words and Music by Jay Livingston
and Ray Evans
Arranged by Glenda Austin

More movement, but with flexibility

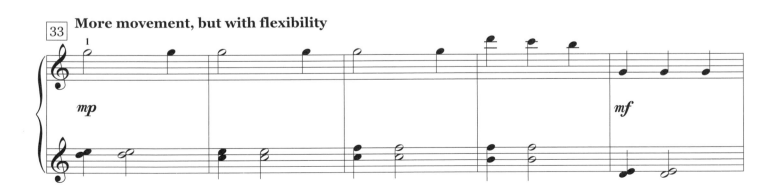

48

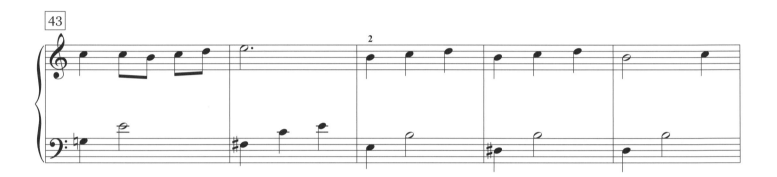

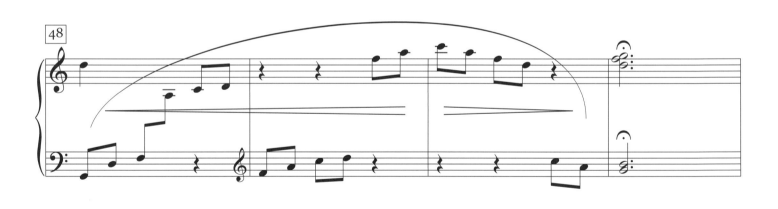

Sleigh Ride

Music by Leroy Anderson
Arranged by Carolyn Miller

Joyously

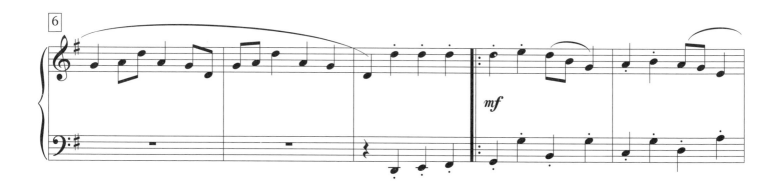

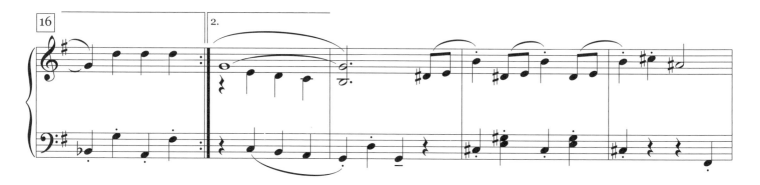

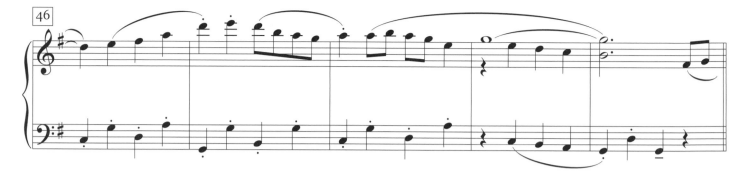

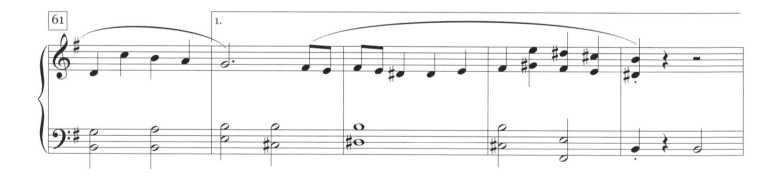

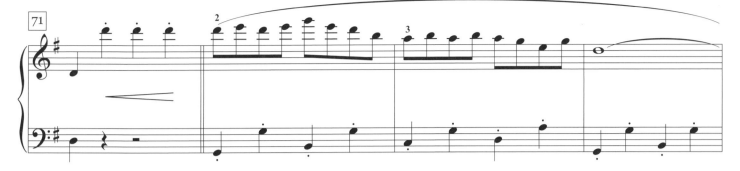

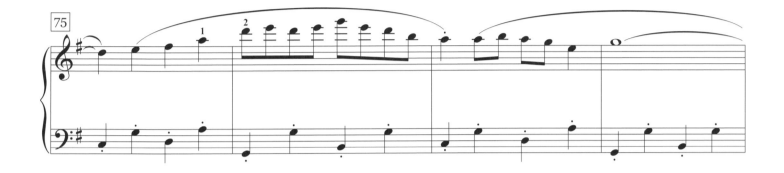

Somewhere in My Memory

from the Twentieth Century Fox Motion Picture HOME ALONE

Words by Leslie Bricusse
Music by John Williams
Arranged by Melanie Spanswick

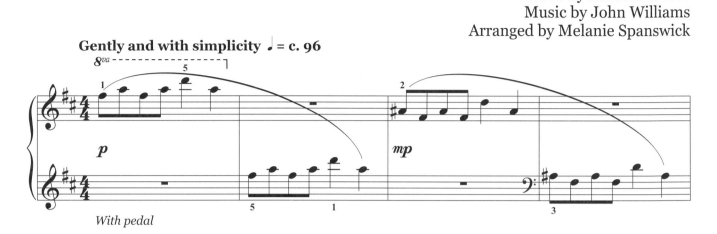

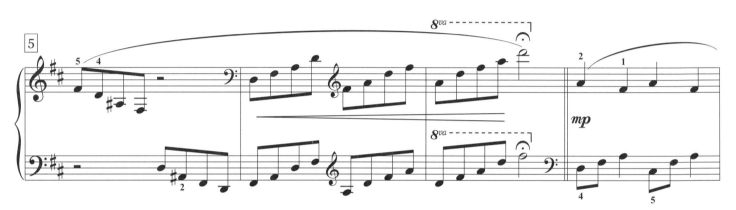

Where Are You Christmas?

from DR. SEUSS' HOW THE GRINCH STOLE CHRISTMAS

Words and Music by Will Jennings,
James Horner and Mariah Carey
Arranged by Melody Bober

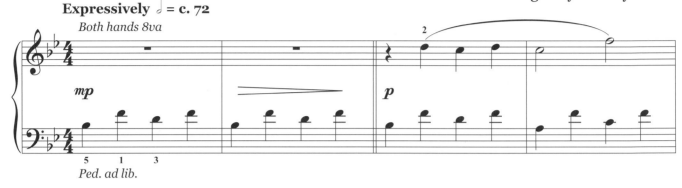

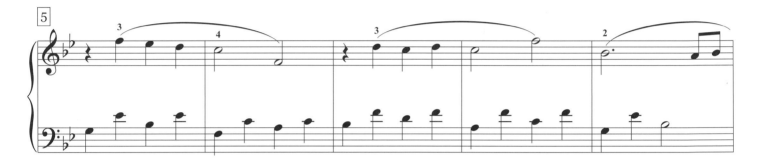

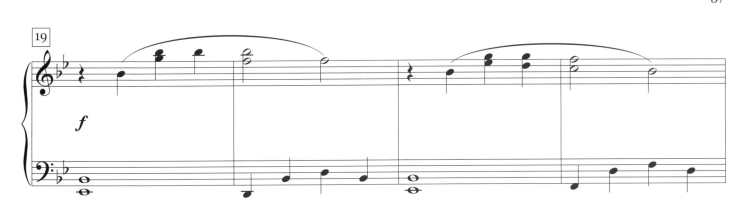

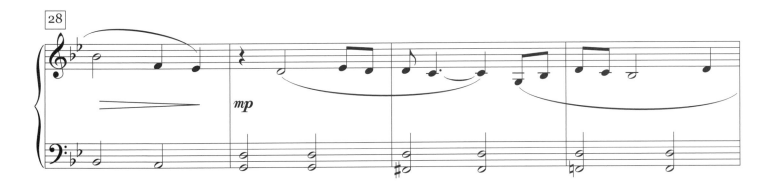

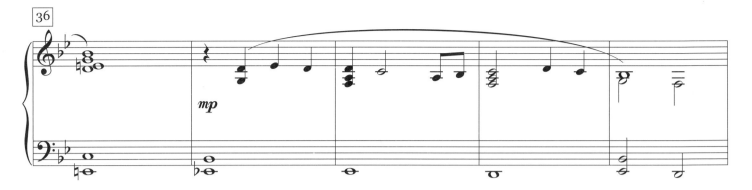

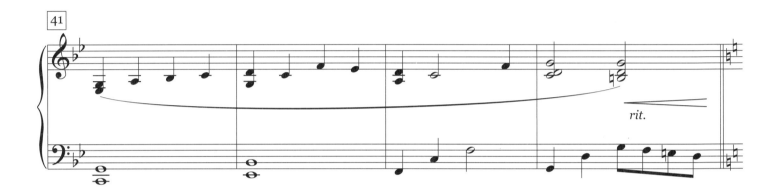

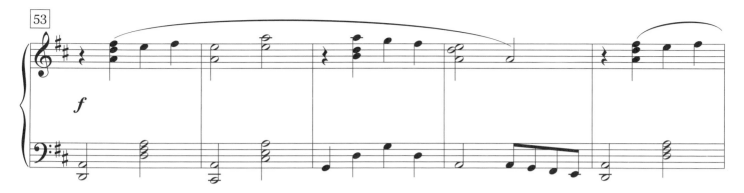

Who Would Imagine a King

from THE PREACHER'S WIFE

Words and Music by Mervyn Warren
and Hallerin Hilton Hill
Arranged by Naoko Ikeda

Gentle waltz

mp

With pedal

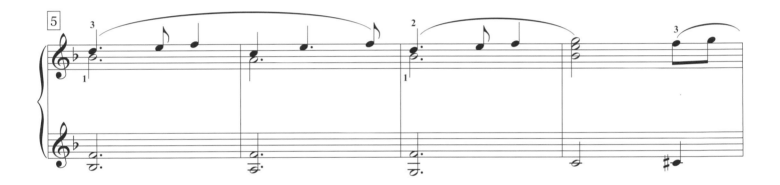

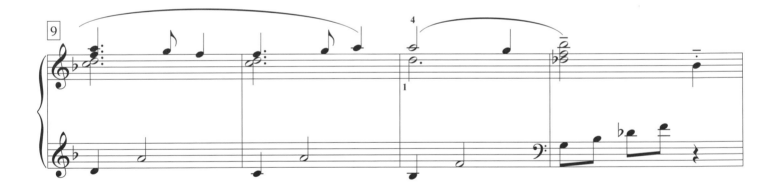

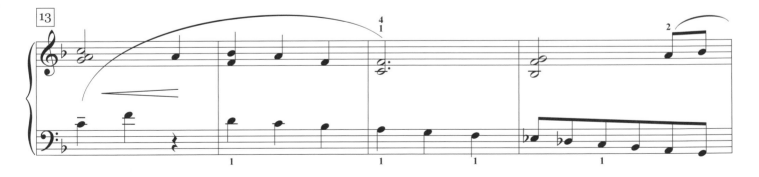

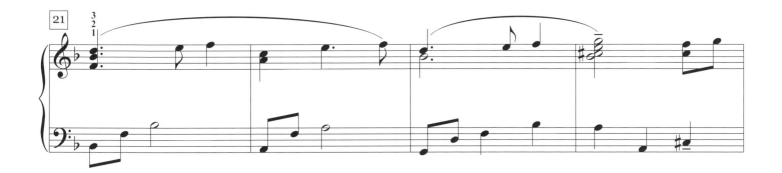

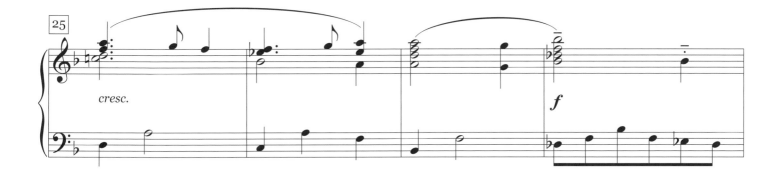

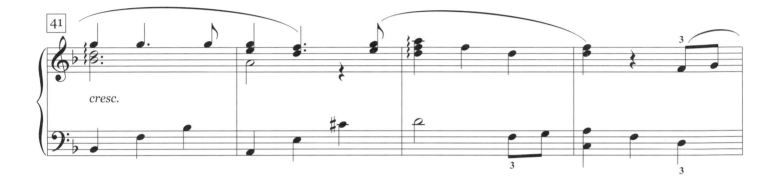

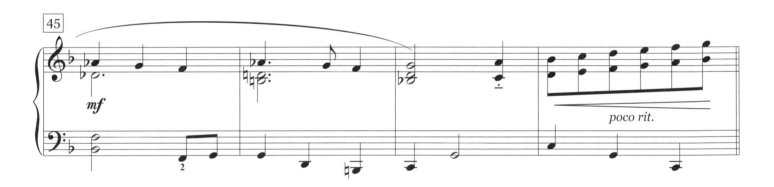

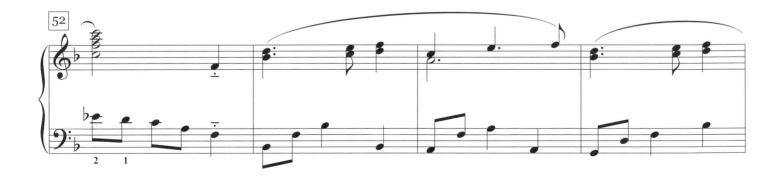

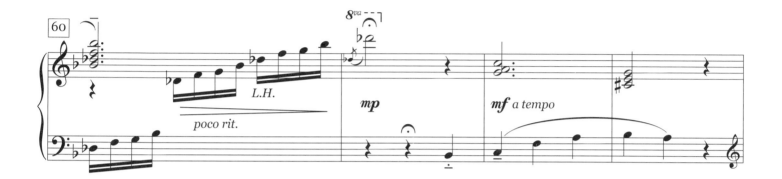

Biographies

GLENDA AUSTIN is an arranger and composer from Joplin, Missouri. During the 2020-21 pandemic she has been performing almost weekly on Facebook Live with the help of her husband David. She would love for you to follow her on YouTube.

ERIC BAUMGARTNER resides in midtown Atlanta with his wife Aretta and their three cats. He has a fondness for a wide variety of musical genres, including jazz, rock, classical, and musical theater.

MELODY BOBER is a prolific composer and arranger from Minnesota and is in great demand as a clinician at conventions and workshops throughout North America.

RANDALL HARTSELL lives in Charlotte, North Carolina and is happily retired from teaching. He enjoys composing, biking, and gardening with his partner Ron.

NAOKO IKEDA is a teacher and composer who lives in Sapporo, a large city in northern Japan that is famous for its snow festivals. One of Naoko's favorite bands is the acapella group Take 6.

CAROLYN MILLER and her husband Gary live in Cincinnati, Ohio. She loves to teach and compose. The late great Regis Philbin once performed two of her pieces on national television!

CAROLYN C. SETLIFF is a teacher and composer from Little Rock, Arkansas. While not the biggest fan of technology, during the pandemic she mastered online teaching.

JASON SIFFORD lives in Iowa City, where he teaches a wonderful group of devoted students, performs regularly with immensely talented local artists, and composes music for his inner child. You can find Jason at www.jasonsifford.com.

MELANIE SPANSWICK is a British pianist, teacher, and composer who lives just minutes from Windsor Castle, the main residence of the Queen. She has wonderful teaching tips, interviews, and blogposts on her website www.melaniespanswick.com.